SO-ADI-598

In the
Presence

THE SPIRITUALITY
OF EUCHARISTIC
ADORATION

Sr. Joan Ridley, OSB

 Liguori

ONE LIGUORI DRIVE
LIGUORI MO 63057-9999

Published by Liguori Publications
Liguori, Missouri
To order, call 800-325-9521
www.liguori.org

Imprimi Potest:
Thomas D. Picton, C.Ss.R.
Provincial, Denver Province
The Redemptorists

Copyright © 2010 Benedictine Convent of Perpetual Adoration

All rights reserved. No part of this publication may be reproduced, stored in a retrieval system, or transmitted in any form or by any means except for brief quotations in printed reviews without the prior written permission of Liguori Publications.

Library of Congress Cataloging-in-Publication Data

Ridley, Joan.
   In the presence : the spirituality of eucharistic adoration / Joan Ridley. -- 1st ed.
      p. cm.
   Includes bibliographical references.
   ISBN 978-0-7648-1907-0
   1. Lord's Supper--Adoration. 2. Spiritual life--Catholic Church. I. Title.
   264'.02036--dc22

                                                                                    2009052710

Unless otherwise noted, Scripture texts in this work are taken from the *New American Bible with Revised New Testament* © 1986, 1970 Confraternity of Christian Doctrine, Washington, D.C. and are used by permission of the copyright owner. All Rights Reserved. No part of the *New American Bible* may be reproduced in any form without permission in writing from the copyright owner.

Where noted, Scripture citations are from the New Revised Standard Version of the Bible, copyright 1989 by the Division of Christian Education of the National Council of Churches of Christ in the USA. All rights reserved. Used with permission.

Liguori Publications, a nonprofit corporation, is an apostolate of the Redemptorists. To learn more about the Redemptorists, visit Redemptorists.com.

Printed in the United States of America
14 13 12 11 10   5 4 3 2 1

First edition

"Receiving the Eucharist means adoring the One whom we receive. Precisely in this way and only in this way do we become one with him. Therefore, the development of Eucharistic adoration…was the most consistent consequence of the Eucharistic mystery itself: only in adoration can profound and true acceptance develop."

POPE BENEDICT XVI

"Christians know that God is everywhere; they know that the whole world is the cathedral where he is eternally adored. And they know that the God who is everywhere present in power and in love has, because we are not always near him, created a few places and realities that make it easier for us, prisoners of space and time, to reach his presence."

KARL RAHNER

Contents

Introduction

If you want to deepen your prayer, these pages may give you encouragement. If you wonder whether eucharistic adoration has any place in the lives of followers of Jesus today, this book may open new channels of insight. If you are drawn to pray in the presence of the exposed Blessed Sacrament, it may ground your experience in the best theology of the Church. If you are a new member of the Church or a catechist or in adult faith formation, you may find a simple yet solid explanation.

It was with this variety of persons in mind that I wrote this small book, but it first grew out of personal experience. After thirty years as a Dominican in a missionary congregation dedicated to the Eucharist, and serving the poor in ministry as a social worker and attorney, I responded to an inner call to embrace contemplative monastic life. In such a life, the main ministry is prayer. The community to which I transferred in 1996, the Benedictine Sisters of Perpetual Adoration, has had a dedication to and practice of eucharistic adoration for all of its 135-plus year history. The eucharistic focus of this congregation is clearly adoration, different from the focus of my former congregation. Over the next twelve years, I received a wonderful gift as I watched my sisters pray and listened to them speak of their love for Jesus Christ in the Eucharist. Gradually, I absorbed an appreciation of adoration. Beyond that, something in me wanted to explore the meaning of adoration that is broader than any one expression such as perpetual adoration. Somewhat to my surprise, as I read and prayed, I found that the theology and spirituality I had first studied after the close of Vatican II provided rich soil for contemporary expressions of prayer *in the presence* of the Blessed Sacrament. They also provided an expanded vision of Christ living in his body, the Church, and in each of its members.

Here are some connections I discovered. Just as the liturgical theology of Vatican Council II enriched our understanding of the celebration of the Eucharist, revitalizing the Church through celebration in the languages of the people and with more participation by all, so today there is a comparable development in eucharistic adoration. Revitalized theology and practice inform each other and continue to renew the Church—and this is happening largely because the people of God are increasingly engaged in the prayer of adoration.

Contemporary eucharistic theology emphasizes relationship, communion, and presence. These dimensions have also renewed the spirituality behind the practice of eucharistic adoration, making it more appealing to modern Catholics of wide diversity in age and culture.

Chapter One

Ancient and Essential Meanings

A woman walked into a church and wondered what was going on. In silence, fifteen or twenty persons were sitting or kneeling in various places throughout the body of the church. There were several who looked college age, and some were elderly. Several were black and several Asian. One person was kneeling in the aisle up front. There was no service going on, but something had their attention. What was it? Then she noticed on the altar the large white host in a gold frame, positioned over a chalice. Those who were praying demonstrated that there was more here than met the eye. She asked someone what was happening and was told this was adoration of Christ in the Eucharist.

Indeed, there *is* more here than meets the eye. When we sit in silence in the presence of the Blessed Sacrament, we are being gazed upon by the Lord. Actually this is true every moment of our lives, but in church or chapel, we have intentionality in gazing at the Lord. That is why we are there. It is an experience of adoration. We do not have to be rationally aware of this reality. It does not depend on our mind so much as our heart.

Adoration

Adoration is our fundamental stance before God, the essential act of relating ourselves to the Absolute. It involves worship. We worship and adore God alone. "But, in what exactly does adoration consist and how is it manifested? Adoration may be prepared by long reflection, but it ends with an intuition, and, like every intuition, it does not last long. It is the perception of the grandeur, majesty, and beauty of God, together with his goodness and presence, which takes one's breath away" (Cantalamessa, *This is My Body*). In Jesus, God became human. We adore him in the sacrament of his Body and Blood. (See also the *Catechism of the Catholic Church*, 2096–2097 and 2628.)

Scripture

The earliest scriptural allusion to God dwelling with us might be the concept of the *shekhinah*, wherein God's presence remained with the people. In biblical Hebrew, *shekhinah* is used to denote the dwelling or settling presence of God, especially in the Temple in Jerusalem, and also God's presence which traveled with the people (Exodus 40:38—cloud by day, fire by night; see Leviticus 9:23 and Numbers 14:10). This goes very far back in religious history—these early instances of God "dwelling" with the people were 1,500 to 2,000 years before Christ.

In Roman Catholic tradition, we reserve the Blessed Sacrament in a tabernacle. The English word "tabernacle" is derived from the Latin word *tabernaculum*, meaning "tent, hut, booth." The Hebrew word for tabernacle, *mishcan*, is also used in the sense of dwelling place, as in Psalm 132:5: "Till I find a home for the LORD, a dwelling for the Mighty One of Jacob."

God is present everywhere, yet specific holy places are important—places where God's extended or universal presence in all creation becomes perceptible to us. The tabernacle is a point of permanent contact with the Sacred. Like Jacob's ladder (see Genesis 28:12), it joins heaven and earth. Heaven is not so much a place as it is God's transcendent realm penetrating our world—most intensely where the risen Christ is present in the praying and celebrating community—in the sacraments, the Eucharist, and acts of selfless love.

Jesus came to give us Life and to give it abundantly (see John 10:10). At the celebration of Eucharist, we receive and eat the Body and Blood of the Lord and adore that which we receive. Outside of the time of Mass, we adore the permanent presence of Christ that is outside ourselves. Both aspects have a scriptural foundation. Compare John 6:54 ("Whoever eats my flesh and drinks my blood possesses eternal life...") with John 6:40 ("For it is my Father's will that everyone who looks upon the Son and puts his faith in him shall possess eternal life...").

God increases our desire by feeding us on many levels. Seeing and eating both increase our longing. In the book of Sirach we hear: "Come to me, you who desire me, and eat your fill. Those who eat of me will hunger for more, and those who drink of me will thirst for more" (Sirach 24:19, 21 NRSV).

As Jesus prepared for his passion, he prayed and invited his disciples to "Abide in me as I abide in you" (John 15:4 NRSV). Jesus abides with the Church throughout time—in the celebration of the Eucharist (Mass) and in the Blessed Sacrament reserved in the tabernacle; more generally, where two or three are gathered in his name.

There are many passages in Scripture with eucharistic symbolism: Moses bows down and takes off his shoes (adoration) before the bush that does not burn; Isaiah receives a burning coal which cleanses his lips (purification); Elijah eats bread baked under the ashes (nourishment); Simeon receives into his arms the child whom he has longed for (desire); Zaccheus heeds Jesus' request: "I must come to your house" (invitation, welcome, risk, conversion); Thomas touches the wounds of Christ (he sees and believes).

As we encounter Christ in the Eucharist, we are gradually

"conformed" to Christ who is taking shape in us (Galatians 4:19). How does this grace occur? Perhaps it is something like osmosis—the imperceptible movement and gradual assimilation of one thing into another. The Word takes root in us, dwelling in our hearts. In the sacraments, we absorb the attitudes and mind of Christ.

Early Church

The early Church acted on the belief that Christ's presence endured and was not limited to the time of the celebration. This was evident when those present would take the eucharistic bread home for family unable to attend because of illness, or for reception of Communion during the week. Over the course of history, many specific practices involving the Blessed Sacrament emerged, further reflecting this belief in the enduring presence. Chapter Two will explore those practices.

Ignatius of Antioch in the early second century wrote: "Our God Jesus Christ is all the more visible now that he is with the Father." In the fourth and fifth centuries, Saints John Chrysostom and Augustine argued that if the Eucharist is truly the full, real presence of Jesus Christ, and Christ is God, the sacrament deserves the same adoration as we give to God.

The Eucharist is a reversal of expected realities. Normally we assimilate what we eat into our body. Saint Augustine had an experience of prayer wherein Christ said to him: "It is not you (human) who assimilate me (Christ) but it will be I who assimilate you" (*Confessions*). In this eucharistic reversal, the eater becomes the eaten. We are assimilated to the body, mind, and will of Christ and to that of his Mystical Body. (See 1 Corinthians 6:17.)

Framing a Question

For the first theologians in the Church, adoration was not worship of the inactive body of the Lord (as if it was an object or a thing), but always involved the action of our being taken up into Christ's offering of himself to the Father in the event of his death-resurrection. At times we have forgotten this. Any of us might ask the rhetorical questions posed by Rev. James Moroney, executive director of the U.S. Bishops' Committee on the Liturgy: "Isn't eucharistic adoration a relic of a pre-conciliar spirituality which de-emphasizes participation for [visual] observation? Isn't eucharistic worship more akin to private devotionalism rather than public liturgical celebration?" The answer, as Father Moroney went on to write, is that yes, eucharistic adoration is a devotion—that is, not a sacrament. But it is a devotion rooted firmly in the liturgy, which can strengthen the liturgical and spiritual life of the parish. This realization has evolved in the Church over time and is evolving still. Chapters Two, Three, Six, and Seven will explain the value and practices of adoration.

The great theologian, Karl Rahner, SJ, summed up the direction of the Church's gradual expansion of understanding in *The Eucharist: The Mystery of Our Christ*:

Because the Church knows that in this reserved sacrament the Lord is truly and substantially present in flesh and blood, in body and soul, in divinity and humanity, she has increasingly learned to venerate this sacrament of her Lord and to worship it, to embrace it with devotion and love....

Just as we humans know someone more deeply after years of interacting with them, so the Church gradually expanded her appreciation for the reserved sacrament of Christ's body.

Some years ago, as Cardinal Ratzinger, Pope Benedict XVI gave a series of homilies on the Eucharist that reflect his deep spirituality. Considering the Church's experience and growth in appreciation of all dimensions of Eucharist, in *God is Near Us: The Eucharist, Heart of Life*, he said:

The Lord gave himself in bread and wine. Those are things we eat. It was said that the bread is there not to be gazed upon but to be eaten. This is essentially right. But let us just recall: What does that mean, to receive the Lord? That is never just a physical, bodily act, as when I eat a slice of bread. So it can therefore never be something that happens just in a moment. To receive Christ means: to move toward him, to adore him. For that reason, the reception can stretch out beyond the time of the Eucharistic celebration; indeed, it has to do so.

The more the Church grew into the Eucharistic mystery, the more she understood that she could not consummate the celebration of Communion within the limited time available in the Mass. When, thus, the eternal light was lit in the church, and the tabernacle installed beside the altar, then it was as if the bud of the mystery had opened, and the Church had welcomed the fullness of the eucharistic mystery.

GOD IS NEAR US: THE EUCHARIST, HEART OF LIFE

This breathtaking quote shows that for us individually and for the Church as a whole, adoration of Christ in the Blessed Sacrament expresses the gradually acquired fullness of Eucharist. This is also expressed in the *Catechism of the Catholic Church*, 1379. Adoration complements and deepens the effects of Eucharist in those who adore. Adoration is not unimportant or easily discarded. Having said that, it is also true that understandings about adoration of the Eucharist have changed over the years as the Church gradually learned to venerate the sacrament of the Lord. In the following chapters, we will look at the ebb and flow of practices throughout history, including the practice of perpetual adoration and contemporary forms of adoration.

Chapter Two
Ebb and Flow
of Practices

If you think about your life and the things you do regularly, you realize that the reasons prompting your actions—and those actions or practices themselves—have changed over the years. In earlier years, you might have volunteered for service in your local community because it helped your career. Later on, you might do it because of an inner conviction or spiritual prompting. At one time in life, being a well-organized person was of high importance, at other times, not so. The same is true of the way we pray or the manner of our relationship with God. What was emphasized in one "season" of life seems gone in another. Or perhaps something that seemed relegated to the past has suddenly come back. "Ebb and flow" is a phrase that implies back-and-forth movement over time. It isn't just about us as individuals. Each of us is part of the universal Church; collective currents sweeping the Church and our society can help explain how we practice our faith.

There is an integral connection between the development of doctrine and the experience of the Church's practicing faithful. One thing is certain: nothing stays the same for long. Karl Rahner, who died in 1984, put it this way: "The Church has a history that is still far from over, that is difficult to foresee, and that time and again surprises us. This applies also to Eucharistic piety...." What changes have you seen in your own lifetime? Depending on your age, it could be quite a few.

One area of change is found in the Eucharist, specifically the relationship between what the community celebrates in the Mass and the enduring presence of Christ in the Blessed Sacrament. Pope Benedict XVI wrote:

Receiving the Eucharist means adoring the One whom we receive. Precisely in this way and only in this way do we become one with him. Therefore, the development of Eucharistic adoration, as it took shape during the Middle Ages, was the most consistent consequence of the Eucharistic mystery itself: only in adoration can profound and true acceptance develop.

"The most consistent consequence" is the phrase that jumps out. The pope is saying that the development of the practice of adoration over time was consistent with the eucharistic mystery, which we adore in the celebration and, beyond those times, in the Blessed Sacrament.

Although it started almost without being noticed, gradually persons began to venerate and pray to the Lord in the Sacrament, reserved originally for the sick. The earliest instances in the first centuries after Christ were among the hermits and solitaries of the East. In an ancient practice, a bishop would carry the eucharistic species to another diocese where a particle would be consumed in the eucharistic celebration as a sign of unity. In the thirteenth-century Rule for Anchoresses, the nuns were to begin their day with a visit to the Blessed Sacrament.

What we know today as exposition of the Blessed Sacrament originated in the liturgy when the eucharistic bread or cup was held aloft for all to venerate at the consecration, or for each individual communicant, before receiving. Liturgical historian Nathan Mitchell maintains that the eucharistic customs of visits, processions, exposition, and benediction all originated within the evolution of the eucharistic liturgy itself as a way to deepen it.

History and context influence spirituality. The feast and procession of Corpus Christi originated in Belgium in the early 1200s as a way to express devotion to the Eucharist. This began at a time when a heretical group (the Cathars) was preaching that matter was evil. Emphasizing the importance of the "matter" of the Eucharist in transforming the earth upon which it was carried in procession restored some balance in a time of great cultural transition.

The practice known as "Forty Hours" began in Milan around 1527. A parish community would spend forty hours in "watch" with the exposed Blessed Sacrament; there was a rotation as the Sacrament was moved from church to church in the locale. The remote historical basis for this practice was the women "keeping watch" at the tomb of Jesus from Good Friday until the early Sunday hour of the resurrection. Forty Hours was a form of uninterrupted, unceasing prayer, and the relay made it perpetual.

The origins of perpetual adoration had some aspects unfamiliar to us. A specific purpose was often the reason for beginning exposition. An early instance was in Avignon, France: adoration was begun in thanksgiving for the victory of King Louis VII over the Albigensians in 1226. Also common was the practice of a number of churches in a diocese having short periods of prayer before the exposed Blessed Sacrament, organized into blocks of time, resulting in a 24-hour/7-days-a-week pattern. Dioceses were divided into twelve sections (months) and then subdivided into thirty for the days of the month. Each church took one day. The "perpetual" aspect was a communal effort of many churches. This dimension, today, has been lost.

The Council of Trent (1545–1563) included reaction to the challenges posed by the Reformation. To avoid any ambiguity, the document on Eucharist clarified in the strongest terms that worship (*latria*) of the Eucharist is an essential part of the Catholic faith. It also encouraged the practice of public exposition of the Eucharist. After Trent, new forms of eucharistic devotion became widespread; religious communities were founded to promote these practices. In the 1800s, some two hundred congregations were characterized by adoration of the exposed Blessed Sacrament—with my own congregation, the Benedictine Sisters of Perpetual Adoration, being one.

At that time, a primary purpose was to make reparation for the outrages committed against the Eucharist by religious dissidents. Persons spent time in prayer reverencing and adoring the Eucharist, which had been ridiculed or physically attacked. But some congregations adopted the approach of Saint Peter Julian Eymard, who found the emphasis on reparation to be inadequate. He realized that the prayer of a congregation devoted entirely to the Eucharist should take its inspiration from the liturgy and said, "We wish to embrace the Eucharist in all its dimensions."

What about today? Is there not still a need for reparation, though for today's reasons? For instance, we need reparation for the violence done to the poor, to women, to the unborn, and to the earth itself...and other harms. And is there not a need to allow the Lord's continual presence in the Eucharist to change us, we who have a hard time being truly present to others amid the clamor of multi-tasking and our fast-paced life? In adoration, we are changed by being present to the Presence.

As mentioned above, eucharistic practices outside of Mass originated as a way to deepen appreciation of and participation in the central action of the Mass. Until the fifteenth century, there was no question of devotions replacing the centrality of liturgy. But other trends in spirituality had begun which did discourage full participation in the eucharistic celebration and, as such, provide an example of how something good can become harmful. From the twelfth century on, there was an increase in the sense of the majesty and awe of the Eucharist and a corresponding sense of unworthiness of the worshipper. This resulted in a decline in participation to such an extent that few but the priest received Communion at Mass. Instead, visual or "ocular" communion was emphasized: seeing the elements of bread and wine held up at the time of the consecration was the "supreme moment." There are accounts from the middle ages of worshippers leaving one Mass after the consecration so they could rush to see the elevation of the host or chalice at another Mass in a nearby church. That practice was an aberration and did not last long.

Perhaps with the deprivation of direct contact with Christ in the Eucharist, the dimension of Communion outside of Mass was shown by increased contact with the Blessed Sacrament through:

- » Practice of visits
- » Forty Hours devotions
- » Benediction
- » Perpetual adoration

These all reflect a deep hunger for Communion, for the Eucharist. As far as these practices reflected an imbalance, there needed to be a correction. The Church makes such self-corrections all the time. For example, formerly the rubric was to genuflect on two knees when the Blessed Sacrament was exposed. Liturgical revisions around 1970 replaced this with a uniform practice of using one knee or making a reverent bow. Why? The Eucharist, when exposed, is not deserving of more veneration than during the eucharistic celebration or when reserved in the tabernacle. Or consider saints: before Vatican II, in some respects, the cult of saints was more prominent than relationship with Christ. For balance to be restored, the Church needed to de-emphasize saints (some even disappeared from the calendar) and provide better catechesis. And now? Saints are back, in proper perspective.

Regarding adoration in general, some dimensions have fallen by the wayside. We no longer speak of Jesus as the "lonely prisoner of the tabernacle" who needs our visit. Nor do we continue practices begun in monarchical France that resembled a kingly honor guard, where the only posture was kneeling and the monstrance was a high throne. The recommended way to expose the Blessed Sacrament now is in a simple monstrance placed directly on the altar. Some communities use a monstrance that resembles the chalice, with the host positioned above it. This preserves the connection with the celebration of the Eucharist. Whereas Popes Leo XIII and Pius XI emphasized reparation as a focus for adoration, Pius XII, in *Mediator Dei* in 1947, shifted the emphasis to prayer that the whole human family, settling their differences, might find peace and be united in mind and heart. The latter intention was certainly appropriate after the carnage and bloodshed of two world wars.

Current eucharistic theology emphasizes relationship with Christ and the members of his body, which flow from Communion, more than it emphasizes his presence in the eucharistic species alone. This may be why, rather than matching Christ's 24-hour availability in the tabernacle by perpetual adoration, many in the Church have placed their focus on the depth and quality of eucharistic adoration.

Official writings of the Church encourage eucharistic adoration without especially promoting perpetual adoration. This emphasis on union and relationship with Christ flowed from the restoration of Communion as the intended outcome of the celebration, peaking when Pope Pius X restored the practice of frequent Communion in the early twentieth century. It is our Communion with the Lord that is the climax of the liturgy and that must be the focus of eucharistic adoration. In a statement attributed to one of the Fathers of the Church, the Eucharist is not consecrated to be adored, but because it is consecrated, it is adored. Adoration, not the number of hours, is the focus of prayer.

Karl Rahner wrote at length about devotion to the Sacred Heart, which was dear to his heart and to his Jesuit congregation. He recognized that the shape and intensity of devotion to the Sacred Heart had changed over time, particularly after Vatican Council II. It had become far less prominent. Rahner argued that any valid dimension of the Church's life should never completely disappear, but should evolve and change. How does the Church hold on to what is needed, while letting some things go? He suggests that we look at the origin of any devotion, its characteristics and forms over time. Distinguish the essential elements of a particular devotion from forms peripheral to it. For instance, the seventeenth-century style of devotion to the Sacred Heart (promoted by a particular saint) fit that time. Each era needs a form for its own time, because the basic devotion is far deeper—at its core, it comes from Scripture.

Rahner's thoughts can be helpful to us when looking at eucharistic practices. Regarding the Eucharist, John Laurance says: "Adoration of the Eucharist derives ultimately from the Church's earliest understanding that in Jesus Christ the Son of God himself has become human." Christ is divine. He said that he would remain with us; we believe that it is true. The Church will continue to foster forms of adoration that fit the hungers of the people of today. We will let some dimensions ebb, while the core practice of adoration will continue to flow.

Sometimes we have a tendency to look back and judge the past as much better than the present. Change can bring balance and welcome development, or it can bring distortion of belief or commitment. It is not easy to describe, especially in the midst of it. Today we are re-discovering the enduring aspects of eucharistic adoration, a practice that the Church had grown into, then downplayed, and then nearly lost.

Chapter Three

Reclaiming
What Endures

Five years after the close of Vatican Council II, a religious sister wrote: "How does God want to be adored as time goes on? We do not know. As the Liturgy continues to develop and to blossom out into richer forms of worship, adoration of the Blessed Sacrament will come into its own. We must remain open to the Spirit and not tie ourselves to means that have been chosen. We must prepare for changes."

Indeed, a great amount of change took place after Vatican Council II ended in 1965. Its official documents confirmed the directions biblical and liturgical theology had taken during the previous thirty years. They emphasized the centrality and breadth of the celebration of Eucharist—the altar of sacrifice is also table of the meal. Additional aspects of Christ's presence were highlighted:

» ...in the people of God gathered as the eucharistic assembly.

» ...in the Word of the Scriptures.

» ...in the presiding minister.

Finally, the revised liturgy restored full participation to the laity. For everyone, this meant attentive entering into the full meaning of their liturgical actions via careful listening, responding, and singing (in their own language), and uniting with Christ and his body, the Church. Additionally, lay Catholics were permitted to assume liturgical roles such as lectors, leaders of intercessory prayer, and ministers of Communion.

As a corollary, other eucharistic practices were de-emphasized. One writer commented that in the 1970s, there was "an immensely significant shift in spirituality from paraliturgy to the Mass, which was increasingly expected to satisfy all our religious needs. Add the ecumenical dimension of worship, which made eucharistic adoration appear a divisive form of prayer, and many could plausibly assert that the traditional forms of eucharistic piety were dying or dead." In the period immediately after the Council, various factors in parishes and religious communities contributed to a lessening or disappearance of eucharistic adoration. This continued through the 1980s. In its place, a broader concept was embraced: adoration as a way of life, explained as being perpetual in that sense. The goal was to adore Christ in all persons, in all of life.

But precisely at the point when eucharistic piety seemed dead, something new began to emerge in the Church, what you might call eucharistic adoration "in a different key." It attracted whole new groups of worshippers. It looked and felt different. Forms of adoration such as Benediction, which depended upon and emphasized the role of the clerical leader in a parish, were not so prominent. Some parishes began perpetual adoration, which prior to this had become a practice almost exclusively within religious congregations. In a fine book, *The Master Is Here: Biblical Reflections on Eucharistic Adoration*, Brian McNeil, CRV, shares his perspective of what he saw happening:

> *All over the world today, we are experiencing a quiet but vigorous flowering of eucharistic adoration. Parishes rediscover it; young people discover it for the first time....Exposition has been detached from benediction...and this means that the Blessed Sacrament can be exposed by women and men religious or even, in some new spiritual movements in the Church, by individual laypersons or groups in small house-chapels. An enormous declericalisation has taken place....*

Eucharistic adoration that we experience today is not exactly the same practice as sixty years ago. There has been a gradual evolution that roots adoration in *this* time period, more fitting for the faith life of today's believers.

A Benedictine nun from England's Stanbrook Abbey describes the desires of young people she encountered:

We are aware of the centrality of Eucharistic Adoration in the New Ecclesial movements and religious orders such as the Jerusalem Community where young people seem attracted by eucharistic adoration. In parishes there has been a marked renewal of this form of worship.... The change in name, from "exposition" or "Benediction" to "eucharistic adoration" is significant, a shift away from what the president of the assembly does to the action of the assembly itself. In recent entrants and those interested in monastic life, [there is a] deep hunger for the presence of Christ in the Blessed Sacrament—the need for silence, the need for focus and simplicity in a world bombarded by a multiplicity of images.

What these voices seem to be emphasizing is that there is a new movement in the Church regarding eucharistic adoration, with its origin in the changing circumstances of the believing community. This is quite different from what some people fear as going backwards, trying to turn back the clock, or a rejection of Vatican II's renewal. It is restoration. When asked what the word "restorationism" meant, then Cardinal Ratzinger—now Pope Benedict XVI—offered a powerful insight: restorationism does not mean a return to the past which, he said, would be undesirable—but it refers to a recovery of lost values within a new totality. Our new totality is the post-modern world with its array of gifts and challenges, never before experienced. Reclaimed or restored practices teach us how to live permanent values, but in a new way. Karl Rahner wrote: "As history goes on, something ancient can again become new, can instruct and inspire later history. That is why, if we wish to create a new future, we may have to return to the sources." Indeed, one of the central calls from Vatican Council II was to return to our sources.

In recent years there has been a "reclaiming" of the practice of eucharistic adoration in the Church. We can ask two questions:

1. How is a practice reclaimed? There are at least two ways. The believing community can find new meanings in old forms (such as re-emphasizing the connection between the celebration of Eucharist and adoration of the Blessed Sacrament outside of Mass) or innovate within the form (borrow from custom to create a new tradition more significant for today). It may be that the style of eucharistic adoration today includes both of these aspects.

2. By whom has eucharistic adoration been reclaimed? It seems to me that it is the people of God themselves, prompted by the Spirit and with some encouragement from official writings of the Church. These documents are consistently strong in saying that adoration, when linked to the celebration of the Eucharist, is an appropriate and core component of the Church's spirituality. Here are two examples, the first from the *Catechism of the Catholic Church:*

"In his Eucharistic presence he remains mysteriously in our midst as the one who loved us and gave himself up for us, and he remains under signs that express and communicate this love: The Church and the world have a great need for Eucharistic worship. Jesus awaits us in this sacrament of love. Let us not refuse the time to go to meet him in adoration, in contemplation full of faith, and open to making amends for the serious offenses and crimes of the world. Let our adoration never cease (CCC 1380).

And from the U.S. Conference of Catholic Bishops:

The celebration of the Eucharist in the sacrifice of the Mass is "truly the origin and purpose of the worship that is shown to the Eucharist outside Mass." Eucharistic adoration extends Holy Communion in a lasting way and prepares us to participate more fully in the celebration of the Eucharistic mystery.

Both of these texts are supportive of adoration because it deepens our faith and enhances our participation in the Eucharist. But whether or not the average Catholic is aware of such "official pronouncements," eucharistic adoration has "caught fire" among the people of God in diverse situations and locations. It might be helpful to summarize reasons why this prayer is finding new life in the Church.

Eucharistic adoration fosters a central dimension of Christian life: adoration itself.

Adoration is a core dimension of our faith, of most any faith. Few have expressed the longing for God that is part of our basic humanity more powerfully than Pierre Teilhard de Chardin in *The Divine Milieu*: "What I cry out for, like every being, with my whole life and all my earthly passion…is a God to adore. To adore…to offer oneself to the fire and the transparency…and to give of one's deepest self to that whose depth has no end." Quite simply, we adore God because our inner being needs to.

Eucharistic adoration deepens our relationship with the person of Christ.

The food we receive in Communion at the celebration of the Eucharist is not a thing but a person, Jesus Christ. This reality remains as long as the eucharistic species do. As in any relationship with a person we love, informal visiting and conversation deepen our love and appreciation of the other. Karl Rahner articulated a theology of "spiritual communion" and said that prayer before the Blessed Sacrament is an instance where it has intense meaning. He links spiritual communion to the same theological reality as "baptism of desire"—which gives the grace of baptism to the person who desires baptism but is unable to be baptized according to the official sacramental rite. Grace is similarly conveyed when a believer experiences genuine repentance in his or her heart outside of any formal sacramental setting. Rahner says that spiritual communion is no less an actualization of our existing unity in Christ, and the "communion" is real, true eating—because it is based on faith.

Consistently, Pope Benedict XVI speaks of the connection between adoration and vital Church life: "Adoration outside Mass prolongs and intensifies all that takes place during the liturgical celebration itself…and strengthens the social mission contained in the Eucharist, which seeks to break down…walls that separate us from one another." Benedict links the practice of adoration with the mission of the Church in its work for social justice.

Eucharistic adoration is a particularly contemplative form of eucharistic prayer.

When people speak of their experience in prayer before the Blessed Sacrament, intimacy with the Lord and a silent listening are often primary. Places of stillness and quiet are almost totally absent today; noise intrusion is constant. Many of us have had the experience of being trapped in a hospital waiting room with a non-stop barrage of CNN or "reality" TV. We also suffer from the racket of public cell phone conversations, electronic bleeps of all kinds, car stereos, sirens, and more. Given this, is it any wonder that contemplative forms of prayer are flourishing?

Adoration is a form of prayer that is largely silent and leads to contemplative prayer. The encounter with the eucharistic Christ flows from the theological principle that the objective and sacramental aspect of the Eucharist must become subjective, personal, and real for each of us who believe. Adoration deepens in us the communion that happens in the celebration of the Eucharist and in other instances of daily life. Contemplation is the means with which we "receive" the mysteries; with which we interiorize them and open ourselves to their action; a way of allowing the grace, received in the sacraments, to mold our inner universe: our thoughts, affections, will, memory. While this can be done at all times and in all places, the place of Christ's uniquely real presence confers immediacy and efficacy. Eucharistic adoration is an occasion to let the heart of Mass—encounter with the risen Christ in bread and wine—become the "continuing object of our thought and gaze" and invite us to deeper, more conscious participation in the meal (Brian Daily, SJ, "Adoration of the Blessed Sacrament").

Eucharistic adoration balances the prominence of "word" with "silence."

Brian Daily notes that Vatican II corrected post-reformation imbalances which in turn led to new imbalances. Our liturgy now has an abundance of words, with little silent prayer; an emphasis on community formation, rather than adoration of God. Further, it seems that some presiders at Eucharist are themselves uncomfortable with more than a few brief moments of silence in the liturgy. Yet silence is a key part of liturgy, along with word, song, symbol, and action. James Moroney, executive director of the U.S. Bishops' Committee on the Liturgy, put it this way: "We live in a society which values 'doing' but doesn't see much value in reflecting and meditating on the mysteries we celebrate. However, without such reflection, we shall not celebrate fully." Most of us know this at least in our heads; we all need to take time to reflect and expand our awareness of God's invitation and action in our lives—which we celebrate in the sacraments and intensify in adoration.

Eucharistic adoration strengthens the celebration.

This is the heart of the matter, since eucharistic adoration is so intimately connected with the celebration of Eucharist. Adoration flows from it. Hopefully we will better participate in the eucharistic celebration because we spend time in adoration. The intrinsic connection may be apparent to the believer who prays, or it may not be. Catechesis is important so the believer who prays in silent adoration can invite Christ's love to expand his or her heart, uniting with Christ's offering of self, perpetuated in the celebration of the Eucharist.

By the late 1970s, Cardinal Ratzinger had begun to realize that concentration on the celebration alone "was causing faith and sacrament to lose something of their place among us....Confined to the space of the sacred rite, Eucharist was becoming a tiny island of time on the edge of the day....The adoration of the sacrament was not in competition with the living celebration of the community, but its condition, its indispensable environment. Only within the breathing space of adoration can the eucharistic celebration indeed be alive..." (*God is Near Us: The Eucharist, Heart of Life*). Adoration is a crucial means by which the action of the celebration is further inserted into our lives.

Experience has shown that eucharistic adoration will flourish within a parish where its life of worship is vibrant—where the celebration of Eucharist and other sacraments are vital, where there are good RCIA programs, and where the focus of eucharistic prayer is the needs of the parish and the world.

A Closing Anecdote

Killian McDonnell, OSB, theology professor at St. John's University, traveled to France in 1988 to address a large gathering of covenant communities. He was impressed by the quality of the Liturgy of the Hours and the Eucharist, and was furthermore surprised to find a tent where twenty-five to one hundred fifty people at a time were praying quietly throughout the day before the exposed Blessed Sacrament. He began to wonder: "Had we dismissed the practice of exposition too lightly after Vatican II?" He returned to the monastery at St. John's and, with some hesitation, shared this experience and question with the renowned liturgist, Godfrey Diekmann, OSB, who shocked McDonnell by saying he agreed with him 100%. Diekmann told McDonnell, "Eucharistic exposition and adoration are nothing else than the action of the Mass held in contemplation" and expressed "mild astonishment that eucharistic exposition should have presented a problem."

What the incident related by McDonnell shows is that we may think eucharistic adoration or exposition of the Blessed Sacrament is a "thing of the past" and have long ago decided it was not part of the contemporary Church. However, mightn't our opinion change when we see how people pray and find meaning in adoration, or how it can be balanced with good liturgical prayer and celebration?

Chapter Four

Varieties of Religious Experience

Prayer is an intensely intimate experience, hardly describable. It can float on the surface, seemingly rote, or plunge to a depth where one's self-disclosure goes far beyond what one's rational mind seems to know. All prayer is a reaching out, a yearning for union with God; at times one senses contact with the Divine, at other times, nothing. Adoration is a specific mode of prayer. Adoration is the prayer of a creature aware of the godliness of God, of the vast distance between them that is real but never a barrier.

Here, we will examine two aspects of adoration—first, that it is ecclesial prayer (prayer of the Church), even when engaged in by one individual; second, that it is about relationship. The book, *Real People, Real Presence: Ordinary Catholics on the Extraordinary Power of the Eucharist,* is aptly titled. In it, about fifty persons share short descriptions of what Eucharist has meant in their lives. Some describe prayer; some connect life events; all share how they have been affected and changed by contact with the Eucharist, usually deepening over time. Their simple prose reflections show God's grace at work in this sacrament of Christ's transforming presence. There are common threads of experience when people describe what Eucharist and adoration means to them. First, Eucharist is about the transformation of our attitudes and actions into those of Christ—in the Benedictine tradition we speak of this as *conversatio*. Second, Eucharist leads us back and forth between celebration and the more contemplative times of adoration. Finally, Eucharist is a gift that builds up the Church, Christ's body, in a very personal way.

Adoration is ecclesial prayer.

All prayer is of equal value, if prayed with faith and attention. However, not all prayer can be called ecclesial—the official prayer of the Church. The sacraments, the celebration of the Eucharist, and the Liturgy of the Hours are examples of ecclesial prayer, which is a focused participation in the paschal mystery. We are plunged into the death and resurrection of Christ and into the body of the Lord, the Church.

Adoration of Christ in the Eucharist is a form of ecclesial prayer because of its intrinsic relationship with the eucharistic celebration. Nathan Mitchell notes that Vatican documents have referred to the Blessed Sacrament as a "permanent sacrament." When we visit the Blessed Sacrament, the enduring fruit of the liturgical action, we make contact not only with the Lord but also with the assembly, God's people. However personal the time before the Blessed Sacrament seems to the individual believer, there is always a social dynamic present that leads the believer back to the Lord's Table. Cardinal Ratzinger expressed it this way: "Whenever we pray in the eucharistic presence, we are never alone. Then the whole of the Church, which celebrates the Eucharist, is praying with us." Eucharistic devotions are not designed so much for expressing personal piety but are meant to renew the assembly itself and intensify participation in the Mass.

The eucharistic liturgy itself shows us what constitutes true Christian adoration: offering ourselves to God within the offering of Christ. We are human, however, and must realize that Christ's self-gift is total, but ours is not. Gradually we "become" the body of Christ in an ongoing reality. Christ's reserved presence remains to draw us ever deeper into his self-gift.

The eucharistic liturgy is a prayer of thanksgiving and offering primarily directed to God the Father. Adoration is a prayer directed to the Lord Jesus and it helps us continue the transformation offered us in Communion during the celebration. Adoration also nourishes us in a different way. Here is how one woman described it:

We in procession (for Communion) consume the precious gift of Christ himself. We are in total communion with each other, and I have a wonderful feeling of belonging. Now I can be Christ to all I meet. But there is another thread to this story. As whole and as joined as I feel when I receive Christ at Mass, there is another way the Eucharist works in my life. This happens in the more private devotion of eucharistic adoration. I am fed in a totally different way when I am lost in veneration of the Lord....

All ecclesial prayer moves in one direction—to transform our minds and hearts into those of Christ. It is God's powerful action at work in our very own lives. The goal of prayer is to transform believers into persons who live what they pray continuously. Here are three examples:

» Participation in the celebration of the Eucharist is meant to lead us to live the Eucharist.

» Liturgy of the Hours (prayer at regular times throughout the day) is meant to lead us to constant praise of God.

» Adoration before the Blessed Sacrament is meant to lead us to a life of continuous adoration.

We need to engage in specific times of prayer so that this transformation may gradually take place. It isn't so much that God needs our prayer but that we need to pray if we are to become the persons God calls us to be.

Finally, the symbols of the eucharistic celebration need to be evident in eucharistic adoration—to maintain the connection. Church documents recommend that when exposed for veneration, the Eucharist be placed on the altar, the table of the meal. When the community gathers for adoration, words of Scripture are to be proclaimed, as they are in any sacramental action. And, while not strongly promoted, some writers have suggested that because of the restoration of the communion cup for all at the eucharistic celebration, exposition could sometimes include both the Body and Blood of the Lord.

Adoration is relational prayer.

In the Eucharist, God comes close to us. God engages in what John Paul II called an act of "Divine condescension," which he contrasted with "inaccessible transcendence." Rather than relating to us only "from the heights," God embraces our human condition, going so far as to transform matter into himself so that we may be so transformed as well. This sets up a profound possibility for relationship. Adoration is the fruit of that relationship. One of the sisters in my religious congregation, Sister Natalia, once wrote: "It should be just as natural for us to adore as it is for a flower to bloom. We find the meaning of adoration in Him whom we adore." In a homily, Cardinal Joseph Ratzinger used a lot more words to speak of this same relationship:

Communion and contemplation belong together: a person cannot communicate with another person without knowing him. Love or friendship always carries within it an impulse of reverence, of adoration. Communicating with Christ therefore demands that we gaze on him, allow him to gaze on us, listen to him, and get to know him. Adoration is simply the personal aspect of Communion. We cannot communicate sacramentally without doing it personally. Sacramental Communion becomes empty, and finally a judgment for us, unless it is repeatedly completed by us personally.

This strikes me as a radical statement: entering into life with Christ in the sacraments must be a highly personal act, completed by personal prayer in relationship. Eucharistic adoration is innately connected with the communion we experience in the eucharistic liturgy.

We may also view adoration from the human developmental process. As we mature, so does our capacity for relationship. Children may relate to each other out of their needs, testing the responses of others. Adolescents enter into relationships that are often marked by insecurity or instability. Adults are capable of serving their families and the broader community in selfless ways. As we grow in faith, we mature as well. We move from only knowing about God to experiencing God. We begin to speak heart-to-heart with the One whom we increasingly love and desire to give ourselves to. We move from acquaintance to friendship and from friendship to intimacy. We cease to be afraid. We can trust God. We become vulnerable, exposing our wounds to the power of the One who has exposed his wounds to us in love. We show the truth of ourselves without protective covering. In Communion, Christ's flesh becomes ours. In adoration, the Christian offers his or her body, the whole self, to the Lord to "take and eat." Over time, our communion and gift of self continues to be gradually woven into the very fabric of our lives. As that happens, our whole lives witness to what God has done and is doing in the "matter" of each unique life. You might call this evangelical living, an intended outcome of prayer.

Ultimately we pray and adore the Lord because we have accepted the invitation of God to relationship, to a communion of love. One does not have to be Catholic, or even baptized, to respond to God. All people of all times in all places are invited. The responses are as varied as the infinite numbers of those who pray.

Chapter Five

Beginning to Adore

If you are a new member of the Church, or perhaps not even Catholic, or you are Catholic but have just been invited to spend your first period of time in eucharistic adoration, you may wonder: What do I do? How do I pray? What if I can't pray?

First of all, relax. In most ways, adoration is no different than any other type of prayer. It is simply me or you relating with God, with Christ Jesus who is really and totally present in the Eucharist. To think about that is both awesome and comforting. God is awesome. Our realization of being a creature, far distinct from God who created us, gives rise to prayer. But this awesome God desires nothing more than that we be in relationship with him (or her, since you may imagine God more as female than male. Of course God is neither male nor female, but the limitations of our language indicate gender). You may already have a relationship with Christ, begun at an early age and nourished by the sacraments. Or perhaps your first encounter with the Lord was quite recent. It doesn't matter. You pray at home, outside, in the car, or while enjoying nature. You pray for your children, grandchildren, friends, enemies, and for the destitute. You hunger for a world where there is more justice, more love. And now you bring yourself to the Lord Jesus who is present in the Blessed Sacrament.

What happens next is up to the Lord. Just move with the flow, and keep coming back.

When we spend time in adoration, our prayer can include all the movements of prayer that take place in the eucharistic celebration. Everything we do there: giving glory and thanks to God, praying for our beloved dead, praying for reconciliation, offering God our contrition for our bent and broken relationships—all of that has a place in the prayer of adoration. Its spirit and attitude are shaped by the mind and heart of Christ as expressed and celebrated in the Eucharist.

A practical difficulty is how to maintain the attention of prayer in a silent setting. This is not a difficulty just for beginners; it is for everyone. Some persons use a prayer mantra—a few words from Scripture such as "The Lord is kind and merciful" or "Christ have mercy" or a few words of one's own such as "I love you; help me to love you in all things." Others pray the rosary or slowly read passages from Scripture, stopping to dialogue with Jesus about them. But it is important to realize that prayer has no element of "success" and that, even more, what happens in prayer does not depend on what you do. It is said that Saint John Vianney spoke with a man in his parish who told him that when he prayed in the presence of the Blessed Sacrament, all that happened was "I look at him (Christ) and he looks at me." Thomas Merton said something to the effect that in prayer we just need to sit there and let God work on us. How God works on us we will never know and we do not need to understand.

Prayer can be silent or with words such as:

I love you
I worship you
I adore you.

Jesus, I pray
for all people,
of all times,
In all places.

I come before you, Lord Jesus,
> exposed and vulnerable, as you are.

I am here,
> drawn by a desire
> to know you
> more intimately.

I am not worthy.

But you do not demand that I be worthy,
> for your love embraces me
> and those whom I love
> and even those I consider my enemies.

Though I do not always feel it,

I am your child,
> adopted through the grace of your unending love,
>> your self-offering and death,
>> your risen and glorified life.

I am yours...

Lord Jesus, you are God,
>	in whom all things are created,
Yet you are the bread of life upon whom I gaze.

To feed me,
>	you gave your body, blood, soul, and divinity
>	broken and poured out.
You give yourself to me
>	as food and nourishment,
So that I may become
>	food and nourishment
>	for those around me who are hungry.

Through the gift of yourself in Eucharist,
>	I share in your mission
>	by *living* the Eucharist.
I do not understand how this is so,
>	yet I believe you desire this,
>	and your grace is sufficient for me.

Chapter Six

Penetrating Gazes

We look intently—stare at or gaze at something that holds our attention. Whether it is a sunset, an animal, or a person, a thing of beauty or of strangeness—we are caught by what is before us. There is an encounter; something is exposed to our gaze and we are gazed upon. The experience is noteworthy. It stays in our minds.

In the New Testament, several words are translated into English as "gazing" or "beholding," and, in context, often what the person sees causes transformation. An early text is Mark 10:21, where Jesus meets the rich young man. "Jesus, looking at him, loved him and said...." The man receives the gaze and invitation of Jesus to follow his way, and yet turns it down.

In the Acts of the Apostles, there is power in what is seen—it left the viewer speechless. "Then when they saw the man who had been cured standing there with them, they could say nothing in reply"(Acts 4:14). The healed individual was the evidence of healing power. In other instances, the Apostles' intense gaze enabled them to perceive faith that was below the surface: "He listened to Paul speaking, who looked intently at him, saw that he had the faith to be healed..."(Acts 14:9). Amazement, astonishment, and wonder were not far away from such seeing. "When he saw the signs and mighty deeds that were occurring, he was astounded" (Acts 8:13).

But the most striking use of "gaze upon" or "behold" comes in the New Testament during the crucifixion of Jesus. The bystanders, officials, and the women with Jesus all "behold" what is happening. The officials mock him; the bystanders beat their breasts, and the women watch (Luke 23:35, 48–49). Jesus, in the act of self-giving on the cross, is exposed to their gaze. Although absolutely powerless, Jesus redeems all things in that very act. In the Letter to the Hebrews, the Greek word for "laid bare" or "exposed" means something close to bending back the head of a sacrificial victim, ready for the knife. "And before him no creature is hidden, but all are naked and laid bare to the eyes of the one to whom we must render an account" (Hebrews 4:13 NRSV). When Jesus was exposed upon the cross, he was dying. Yet the meaning of it was not determined by his executioners, but by his love and surrender to the Father in the midst of that terror. After the soldier pierces the side of Jesus with a lance, the author of John's Gospel says this was to fulfill Scripture: "They will look on the one whom they have pierced" (John 19:37). The word translated into English as "look upon" is often used when there are appearances of the Lord God in glory, of angels or messengers of God, and of the risen Jesus. (See 2 Corinthians 3:18.)

In everyday secular usage, the word "exposed" is often connected with harm or risk. We speak of being exposed to severe weather, to germs, chemical leaks, or corrupting influences. When the eucharistic species is exposed (during exposition), we gaze upon it. We may not be conscious of this reality, but the Lord takes a risk in being exposed. The risk is our rejection of his love, or worse—ridicule and disrespect.

We who come before the Lord expose ourselves as well. We become both vulnerable and engaged with possibility. In the Scriptures, being exposed is the way to meet the Lord and be healed. Recall two well-known stories. Zacchaeus climbs a tree to see the Lord. Perhaps he did not intend to *be seen*, but he was. He was exposed to the Lord's knowing gaze. Jesus called him down and invited himself to his house. From then on, Zacchaeus' life takes radically different turns towards conversion and justice. In his willingness to welcome the Lord, he realizes how incongruent his life was, and he offers to give his possessions to the poor and to repay fourfold anyone whom he has cheated. (See Luke 19:1–10.)

In Luke 6:19, we are told that a healing power came out from Jesus. A dramatic story is that of the woman with the hemorrhage. (See Mark 5:25–34; Matthew 9:20–22; Luke 8:43–48.) Having suffered for many years, a woman tries to touch Jesus without being known. She desperately hopes for healing. Jesus, sensing that power has gone out from him, asks who touched his clothes. Realizing she has been healed, the woman comes to him, perhaps fearful of exposing herself to his anger. The woman "fell down before him and told him the whole truth" (Mark 5:33). This includes the sadness of her exclusion from ritual prayer due to her hemorrhage and the financial ruin her sickness has caused. Now healed, she can rejoin religious society. Jesus calls her "daughter" and tells her that her faith has made her whole. "Precisely because this is for him a personal encounter," writes Brian McNeil, CRV, "Jesus cannot let the woman simply slip off into the anonymity of the crowd after she has been healed. He has exposed himself to her by allowing her to take hold of his cloak. Now she must dare to expose herself to him, for otherwise she would not advance beyond the initial level of faith...." The woman wanted healing, perhaps a "magical" kind with no personal encounter. But by calling her forward to explain her action, Jesus heals her not only physically, but removes her psychological scars as well. The same may be true for us: Jesus wants us to go beyond what we think we want to what we really need.

When we pray with honesty, we expose ourselves to Christ. We hope for healing, we expose our wounds to his penetrating gaze, and tell him the whole truth. He sees us as we are, without any protective covering. A privileged place for this to occur is in the presence of Christ, exposed to us in the Blessed Sacrament. In a more general description of prayer outside of the eucharistic context, Timothy Radcliffe,

OP, had this to say: "To be seen by Jesus is an experience of truth. Think of the Samaritan woman at the well: 'He told me all that I ever did' (John 4:39)....Jesus' delight in us is not a vacuous affirmation: it is our painful joy in being stripped of pretension, of stepping into the light. In the presence of that face we discover who we are." We must dare to be exposed to his view, confident that he will delight in us. The dimension that Radcliffe highlights is that when prayer is a real meeting at our depths with Jesus, we come to know both our true self and that God takes delight in us. This is a truly liberating experience.

Liturgy is meant to nourish faith, using all our senses. Some parts of liturgy are heard (for example, the name of God, listening to the Word of God); some are visual (for example, icons). Exposition is an example of a *visual* reality. In the western Church, exposition of the Eucharist mirrors the eastern devotion to icons. In my monastery, Sister Carmela Rall writes icons and can attest to the emerging desire of many western Christians to use icons in their prayer. She says: "Praying with an icon is contemplating the Word of God in color. In order to pray, to communicate or to gaze at an icon, the body, mind, and spirit must seek quiet, silence, and solitude." Icons help us sense the closeness of God and the events, persons, and mysteries portrayed in them. There need not be a liturgy going on when icons are venerated in a church. Those who venerate icons may use candles and pray similar words of praise and love as used in the liturgy and engage in gestures of veneration. Icons serve as points of connectedness—or communion—with the divine. They help overcome our normal inability to see and to sense all that is around us. They point to the reality that we are surrounded by the communion of saints and the constant presence of Christ who is saving us. Exposition of the Blessed Sacrament—by holding our attention—allows the believer to focus on the inner communion with Christ.

We use the "eyes of faith" to see the Master and contemplate him in love. Karl Rahner asks: "When the mystery of Christ always and everywhere encompasses our being...why should this not be allowed to become visible so that our eye may fall on the food of the Church...?" (*The Eucharist: The Mystery of our Christ*). He also points out that "eternal happiness" is presented as seeing God face-to-face, more even than hearing the unfiltered Word. He writes about the power of the visual symbol of the crucifix and of icons. These images say far more than volumes of words could. Nathan Mitchell speaks of "eye centeredness"—the bonding that occurs in the earliest stages of life when a baby begins to see and recognize another person. Among adults, a relationship begins when one person notices another and makes eye contact. It may never develop beyond that, but it has established itself.

Gazing is a contemplative activity. As we sit or kneel before the Eucharist exposed, we are engaged in a particularly Catholic form of contemplative prayer. We learn to gaze lovingly and be gazed upon. God looks on us with mercy and gentle kindness. To adore, according to the wonderful expression of Saint Gregory of Nazianzus, means to raise a "hymn of silence" to God. Deep silence happens when we are in communion with God, who is silence as well as word. Father Franco Sottocornola compares the eastern prayer form, *Zazen*, with eucharistic adoration. In both we are encountering God beyond words and images, in self-emptying. His reflection on God's silence in the Eucharist is quite powerful: "Silence is one suggested form of prayer before the Blessed Sacrament. Too seldom do we stop and listen to the silence of Christ in the sacrament of the Altar preserved in the Tabernacle. The eternal Word of God in His death has become silent….The sacramental silence of the broken bread kept in the Tabernacle of God's presence to us is an invitation to go beyond all words, all imagination and all images, beyond all that divides or separates, beyond all objects to the perfect communion of life and love." In the Eucharist, the Word is silent, as Jesus was silent at his death. After the resurrection, his "voice" is no longer physical, and our images of God must be changed as well. Another link between exposition of the Blessed Sacrament and icons is this silence. The stillness of the icon invites prayer; the exposed Blessed Sacrament is still and silent and invites our attention and prayer. We silently encounter the Incarnate Word in the Eucharist.

Finally, it is important to realize that exposition is a liturgical act, even as it includes silence, even as it sometimes involves only one or two persons at a particular time. It is not just a backdrop for personal prayer. Liturgical regulations say that when the whole community gathers, readings from Scripture and the early Church, songs, and prayers of thanksgiving and intercession are to be used. Why? Well, the elements of liturgical worship focus exposition (worship) of the Eucharist outside of Mass on the event of the paschal mystery (death and resurrection) of the Lord. Like the eucharistic celebration itself, prayer before the Lord's presence is meant to transform us so that we live the Eucharist fully. When we pray in eucharistic adoration, we are engaged in the prayer of the Church. The end result for us is to, like Christ, become "bread broken" for a hungry world. In this way, the Eucharist extends into the cosmos.

Chapter Seven

Into the Cosmos

There is criticism of eucharistic adoration in the Church. It seems partly reasonable, but mainly based on misunderstanding. It is quite true that at times in the history of the Church, emphasis has been misplaced. In the century before Vatican Council II, much popular spirituality and theology had become narrow. This could be illustrated by the title of a once frequently used catechetical series: "Jesus and I." The sacraments were viewed mainly in terms of what took place in the individual. What happened in the eucharistic celebration was primarily seen as between God and the person, lacking any dimension of communion among the members of the worshipping community. The same was true for practices such as eucharistic adoration. Anyone over a certain age absorbed these concepts. Some have never moved beyond this approach, and their spirituality remains focused almost exclusively on the individual dimension. Writings that promote eucharistic adoration sometimes reflect *only* this approach.

Other believers have integrated the theology of Vatican II, which re-inserted the dimension of community, both local and global, into theology. These persons may judgmentally view eucharistic adoration as a relic of the past, as reflective of the individualistic spirituality of recent centuries. They fail to understand that development of doctrine and spirituality has occurred in the practice of eucharistic adoration, just as it has regarding the celebration. There are expansive and complementary dimensions of eucharistic spirituality. There is no dichotomy between the practice of prayer before the Blessed Sacrament and a broad, cosmic understanding of Christ's presence in people and in the cosmos.

"The substantial conversion of bread and wine into [Christ's] body and blood introduces within creation the principle of a radical change, a sort of 'nuclear fission,' to use an image familiar to us today, which penetrates to the heart of all being, a change meant to set off a process which transforms reality, a process leading ultimately to the transfiguration of the entire world, to the point where God will be all in all (cf. 1 Cor 15:28)" (Benedict XVI, *Sacramentum Caritatis*). These words of Pope Benedict XVI echo those of Teilhard de Chardin, with whom a sense of liturgy as cosmic has long been associated. Benedict uses such concepts frequently, showing perhaps that de Chardin's thought has become mainstream in the Church. And, although "nuclear fission" and "cosmic reality" are modern terms, the ancient author of the Letter to the Colossians also spoke of Christ in a cosmic dimension: "He himself is before all things, and in him all things hold together" (Colossians 1:17).

Our liturgy, the celebration of Eucharist, and eucharistic adoration are all part of something much larger than what happens in a building among a group of worshippers. Such worship is part of a larger liturgy that encompasses the whole world. Christ is present in the bread and wine because God has first loved and graced the entire world in Christ. Some years ago, Cardinal Ratzinger put it this way: "Christian liturgy is cosmic liturgy....The eucharistic bread imparts its blessing to the daily bread, and each loaf of the latter silently points to him who wished to be the bread of us all. So the liturgy opens out into everyday life; it goes beyond the church precincts....Liturgy is not the private hobby of a particular group; it is about the bond which holds heaven and earth together, it is about the human race and the entire created world" (*Feast of Faith*). This is another mind-expanding quotation showing that liturgy blesses our daily bread and links the entire human race and created world. Liturgy, worship, and prayer are meant to open us to what God knows—that all things are one and joined together. God's love is world-embracing and so, therefore, must ours be. Karl Rahner once said that "In Jesus God has...become world" (*Eucharistic Worship*). This is so that Christ may "lead the world back into the splendor of God" through the instrument of ordinary matter—bread and wine. God descended into the human condition in order to redeem us; the risen Christ descends further, into humble matter itself, to the level of "things" where he becomes nourishment and joy in bread and wine. What a dynamic and wondrous reality! All things are vehicles of God's salvation—even inanimate matter.

This understanding can transform our attitude towards creation. Far too often, we human beings relate to creation as an oppressed worker against a domineering and despotic overseer. We use the created world for our needs and pleasure without thinking of the consequences. With such an attitude, the universe is not a source of wonderment, but something to be tamed. We can misuse and abuse the earth, taking all of its resources. But when we really set our eyes on the beauty of a new flower or the multitude of stars, we experience a sense of awe. We glimpse God's hand in them. Surgeons and astronauts have reported a change in their attitudes as they come into contact with the intricacy of a blood vessel or the expansiveness of the universe. While all creation has been saved in Christ, it is in the bread and wine that the Lord has fully united creation to himself. Eucharistic adoration—the contemplation of God whose presence transforms the bread and wine—overturns the attitude of domination.

Almost one hundred years ago, Teilhard de Chardin wrote: "Christian prayer should give great importance to the real and physical extensions of the eucharistic Presence...the host is comparable to a blazing fire whose flames spread out like rays all round it" (*Hymn of the Universe*). Cardinal Ratzinger spoke of Christ's body, the Eucharist, as not only uniting with us but also *seizing hold of* one's body, transforming it into his own. Why? So that we may serve the world as Christ did.

Christ's presence is derived from sacrifice. Presence is not an end in itself. Presence is always directed toward sacrifice and extending communion, as Christ did. We are drawn into the paschal mystery, so that we may become an instrument of God's salvation in a mysterious yet real way. This is what is meant by saying that "adoration is a way of life." But it is important to keep in mind that in order for adoration to be a way of life, it is we who must be transformed, and it only happens gradually. Times of eucharistic contemplation foster the transformation and are every bit as important as times of action and celebration. In other words, like so many aspects of life and spirituality, the complete reality is "both/and," not "either/or."

An ancient monastic source of wisdom is the *Conferences of John Cassian* mentioned by Saint Benedict in his Rule. In the first conference, Cassian teaches:

» The "end" or *primary goal* of the spiritual life is *eternal life*—life with God in the hereafter.

» In order to get there, the *intermediate goal* or desired "state of being" on earth is *purity of heart*. This is because one whose heart is pure or purified can see God, as Jesus said.

» The means to achieve purity of heart are those practices one engages in all day such as fasting, vigils, labor, and reading.

Cassian cautions us not to hang onto the practices themselves, but to see them in terms of the goal. But the reverse is also true: means or practices are necessary to achieve the goal.

When we consider eucharistic spirituality:

» Our *primary goal* is union with Christ in praise and adoration of God.
» The *intermediate goal* is a life of adoration.
» The *means* to this goal are the eucharistic celebration and eucharistic adoration.

Both the goal and the means are important. They emphasize the relationship between the eucharistic bread and our daily bread, between liturgy and life. To share in the meal of eucharistic fellowship should prompt us in daily life to give to the poor and, in so doing, invite them to "the table." We want to adore Christ in the Blessed Sacrament on the altar and also see, recognize, and honor his presence in other persons. Both of these examples are saying the same thing—prayer and liturgy are meant to change us so that we become more loving, more like Christ, who cares about and loves every person and all things.

There is a final connection. We cannot move towards our goal of "adoration as a way of life" unless we also spend time in adoration of Christ in the Blessed Sacrament. In *The Eucharist: The Mystery of Our Christ*, Karl Rahner wrote: "The Christian cannot say that the communion of life with God does not need the communion with God under the sacramental sign….The growing consecration of both is the task of our life." Mother Teresa of Calcutta's life and spirituality exemplified the unity of these two realities. "Without the contemplation of the Christ who is hidden under the veil of the sacrament," wrote Brian McNeil, "Mother Teresa and her sisters would not be able to recognize Christ who is hidden under the veil of the outcasts." Pope Benedict emphasizes adoration for the same reason. "Far from being a privatized, ethereal devotion…adoration is a basic posture in life…. Adoration must surely give rise to the service of neighbor, but that service will founder if it loses a sense of wonder before the one who loves us first."

Once again, Pope Benedict links adoration with the social justice mission of the Church. Adoration leads us to serve our neighbor; we who serve need the contemplative times of adoration so that we may persevere.

Just as the eucharistic liturgy enables us to see or sense God's saving action (liturgy) in all of life, so also adoration of the Blessed Sacrament leads us to see and recognize that all things are permeated with Christ. Again, this is a gradual realization. We are in constant need of a renewal of our focus and deepening of our perception, for otherwise they diminish and fade. We are on the way, being drawn towards a future that includes all that has gone before, ever more filled with grace. One ordinary believer described these connections very simply:

There is no place else on earth where the richest and poorest can stand together to receive the most precious of gifts: Christ himself. In the Eucharist, if only for a few moments, I live the body of Christ—one in love with God through his Son, Jesus, and one with my brothers and sisters in that same love. Can I live the sacrament beyond those moments? Can I be a sacrament to others, as the Lord intends?

Chapter Eight
Continuity Into the Future

In previous chapters, we looked at worship of the Eucharist: where it came from, how it evolved, what broad and specific meanings are found in the Church's understanding, and how people pray in the presence of the Blessed Sacrament. "Where do we go from here?" or "The Future" is a final topic to explore. Of course, only God knows! Nonetheless, since there is continuity in experience over time, I can draw together threads explored in previous chapters.

The Church

Patterns of spirituality, prayer practices, devotions, and forms of liturgy change and evolve over time, affecting individuals and the Church as a whole. We are led by the Spirit of God into ever-deeper communion with God. God works with whatever happens to us. We can say that what happens to us over time is that things change.

Recent history has shown that the Church—people of God

and leadership—is not letting eucharistic adoration go by the wayside as it seemed in the 1970s and 1980s. Why not? One explanation is that Vatican II happened right when the culture was moving at warp speed toward extreme secularization. People ended up with a significant loss of contemplative practices and places—silent retreats disappeared overnight. People were hungry for contemplative experience. Many sought that experience in the practices of eastern religions. Others, such as Father John Main, OSB, began to teach Christian contemplative prayer—continuing now through the World Community for Christian Meditation. In the Catholic tradition, people had enough exposure to the new liturgy to come back to adoration with a different mindset, seeing adoration as fluid, as something that flows from and back into the Mass and the community.

There is another reason why adoration didn't die, and it relates to generational differences. The perspective of those who came of age, theologically, just before or after Vatican Council II (1962–1965) is not the same as those who came of age later. Adult Catholics under fifty did not have the pre-Vatican II experience of worship of the Eucharist outside of Mass, whatever its limitations may have been. In contrast, many Catholics have had (an often problematic) post-Vatican II experience: a catechesis that was guided by shifting emphases, sprinkled heavily with balloons and banners, but with too little that nourished their lives for the long haul. In other words, every era has its excesses and imbalances.

For even younger Catholics today, raised in a totally secularized culture, ritual and visible symbols or signs of Catholic identity are important and valued. It may be hard for those over sixty to understand the imperatives of that perspective, just as it was hard for those raised in the Great Depression to understand the perspectives of their offspring. The Church should always be open to emerging forms of practice, because new articulations happen as a result of changes in personal or collective life.

More than twenty-five years ago, when the Church was reclaiming the centrality of the eucharistic celebration, theologian Karl Rahner saw the need not to lose the practice of eucharistic adoration: "Christians know that God is everywhere, that he carries everything with his power and his love, and is incredibly near to everything; they know that the whole world is the cathedral....But these Christians also know that their own adoring love is not always near the God who is always near them. And they know that the God who is everywhere present has created a few places and realities that make it easier for us, prisoners of space and time, to reach his presence" (*Eucharistic Worship*). Yes, God is and can be adored everywhere. But it is we who need the concrete reality of regular prayer and adoration—and the specific place where Christ is present to us in the Blessed Sacrament.

Perhaps we are now living at the intersection of two key questions posed by Father John McKenna, CM. We have, he says, spent the last fifteen to twenty years answering "yes" to the first question:

> » Is it possible to return to the center (centrality of celebration of the Eucharist) without losing the values of eucharistic devotions outside the Mass?

And now we must ask the second question:

> » Is it possible to re-discover the value of eucharistic devotions outside of Mass without letting them again slip loose from their moorings?

By "slip loose from their moorings," I suspect he means that devotions such as adoration could be disconnected from the central sacramental life of the Church, out of sync with the Church's core theology. In order to avoid that, we must make sure that eucharistic adoration is grounded in the eucharistic celebration. That is why prayer forms from the Mass (readings from Scripture, prayers, silence, and song) are used in the ritual for exposition. This is also why, if exposition takes place in the parish church, the monstrance is placed on the altar. Theologically, adoration must be anchored in the spirit of the paschal mystery to link it with the celebration.

Eucharistic adoration has the potential to continue to contribute to renewal in the Church by deepening faith in all those who practice it. Everett A. Diederich, SS, wrote: "From well-celebrated rites of exposition and benediction their hunger and thirst for him will grow. There will be a deeper recognition of him in the next breaking of the bread. The pilgrim Church will be satisfied with the bread of life in communion and find deeper union with him and through him with the Father and each other. He will send his refreshed and renewed ecclesial body forth to feed a spiritually hungry world." Adoration intensifies what the Eucharist is doing in us and sends us forth as loving Christians who feed others.

The Believer

Faith is incarnate in you and I who believe. Ritual is the expression of our faith. Adoration is a particularly contemplative form of eucharistic prayer. It is to be encouraged. However, and this is important, the believer's faith will not be nourished if the Church does not also teach methods of contemplative prayer used in eucharistic adoration. Such methods are silent and affective prayer, how to ponder the Scriptures contemplatively, and an understanding of the stages of spiritual maturation and relationship. We need guidance and direction. Without this, archaic and narrow expressions of eucharistic piety could once again become predominant.

As mentioned in the section on church, the person who adores needs to be steeped in the prayer of the celebration. Thus if I have discovered the inner dynamics of the celebration and let myself be fashioned by the God who gathers, who speaks, who gives himself, and who sends, then my time of adoration of Christ in the Eucharist becomes energized.

The values that the eucharistic celebration inspires should also be found in my prayer of adoration outside the celebration:

» **Communion with Christ**

In adoration: prolong the personal encounter.

» **Adherence to God's Word**

*In adoration: assimilate the
word of God into oneself.*

» **Participation in the Paschal Mystery**

*In adoration: join one's surrender
to that of Christ before the Father.*

» **Thanksgiving and Supplication**

*In adoration: prolong the thanksgiving;
intercede for all persons in all places.*

» **Offering and Gift of the Spirit**

*In adoration: offer oneself, the community,
and our world in Christ so that all is healed.*

The riches that our loving God offers us in prayer centered in the Eucharist are enormous. Prayer is the response of love to one who loves us. It is the cry of need as we stand with and before the Lord Jesus in the sacrament of the altar and pray for all people of all times and all places—bringing with us the specifics of our family, our lives, of everything. The risen Christ remains with us in the Blessed Sacrament and invites us to participate in his mission of unending self-gift that continues to save the world. There is no time like now. The banquet is before us and in us. *Come let us adore.*

Acknowledgments

Cantalamessa, Raniero. *This Is My Body: Eucharistic Reflections Inspired by Adoro Te Devote and Ave Verum.* Pauline Books, 2005.

Catechism of the Catholic Church, Second Edition 1994. English translation for the United States of America copyright © 1994, United States Catholic Conference, Inc.—Libreria Editrice Vaticana. English translation of the Catechism of the Catholic Church: Modifications from the Editio Typica copyright © 1997, United States Catholic Conference, Inc.—Libreria Editrice Vaticana.

Daily, Brian, SJ. "Adoration of the Blessed Sacrament: Contemporary Catholics on Traditional Devotions," *America Magazine,* Vol. 188, No. 13, April 14, 2003.

de Chardin, Teilhard, SJ. *Hymn of the Universe.* Harper and Row, 1965. Copyright © 1961 by Editions du Seuil. Copyright © 1965 in the English Translation by William Collins Sons & Co., Ltd, London and Harper & Row Inc., New York.

———. *The Divine Milieu.* Harper Torchbooks, 1965. Copyright © 1957 by Editions du Seuil. Copyright © 1960 by William Collins Sons & Co., Ltd, London and Harper & Row Publishers, Incorporated, New York.

Diederich, Everett, SJ. "Eucharistic Worship Outside Mass" in *The New Dictionary of Sacramental Worship*, ed. Peter E. Fink. Liturgical Press, 1990. Copyright © 1990 by The Order of St. Benedict, Inc., Collegeville, Minnesota.

Johns, Dame Laurentia, OSB. "Eucharistic Adoration in the Church and in Monastic Life," delivered at English Benedictine Liturgical Symposium. Stanbrook Abbey, 2002. http://www.benedictines.org.uk/theology/2002/index.htm.

Keeler, William H. *Real People, Real Presence: Ordinary Catholics on the Extraordinary Power of the Eucharist.* The Word Among Us Press, 2005.

Laurance, John D. "The Eucharist and Eucharistic Adoration," Louvain Studies, Vol. 26, No. 4, 2001.

McDonnell, Killian, OSB. "Eucharistic Exposition: An Obsolete Relic?" *America Magazine*, Vol. 160, No. 7, February 25, 1989.

McKenna, John M. "The Theology of Adoration," *The New Dictionary of Sacramental Worship* (dictionary noted above).

McNeil, Brian, CRV. *The Master Is Here: Biblical Reflections on Eucharistic Adoration.* Dublin: Veritas Books, 1997.

Mitchell, Nathan D. *Cult and Controversy: The Worship of the Eucharist Outside Mass.* Pueblo Publishing Co., 1982.

Moroney, James. "Eucharistic Adoration Outside of Mass," *Origins*, Vol. 27, No. 36, February 26, 1998. Copyright © 1998 by Catholic News Service/U.S. Catholic Conference.

Pope Benedict XVI. Address to the Curia. December 22, 2005. © 2005 Libreria Editrice Vaticana.

———.*Sacramentum Caritatis* (Post-Synodal Apostolic Exhortation on the Eucharist as the Source and Summit of the Church's Life and Mission). February 22, 2007. © 2007 Libreria Editrice Vaticana.

Pope John Paul II. *Dominicae Cenae* (Letter on the Mystery and Worship of the Eucharist). February 24, 1980. © 1980 Libreria Editrice Vaticana.

Radcliffe, Timothy, OP. *What Is the Point of Being a Christian?* London: Burns & Oates, 2005. © Timothy Radcliffe 2005.

Rahner, Karl, SJ. "Devotion to the Sacred Heart Today," *Theological Investigations Vol. XXIII, Final Writings.* NY: Crossroad, 1992.

———. "Eucharistic Worship," *Theological Investigations, Vol. XXIII, Final Writings.* NY: Crossroad, 1992.

———. *The Christian Commitment: Essays in Pastoral Theology.* Sheed and Ward, 1963. © Sheed and Ward, Ltd., 1963.

———. *The Eucharist: The Mystery of Our Christ*, trans. Salvator Attanasio. Denville, NJ: Dimension, 1970.

———. "The Theology and Religious Meaning of Images," *Theological Investigations Vol. XXIII, Final Writings.* NY: Crossroad, 1992.

Ratzinger, Joseph. *Feast of Faith.* Ignatius Press, 1986. © 1986 Ignatius Press, San Francisco.

———. *God Is Near Us: The Eucharist, the Heart of Life.* Ignatius Press, 2003. © 2003 Ignatius Press, San Francisco.

Sottocornola, Franco, SX. "Zazen and the Adoration of the Eucharist," *Japan Mission Journal*, Spring 1995.

United States Conference of Catholic Bishops, Bishops' Committee on the Liturgy. "Thirty-One Questions on Adoration of the Blessed Sacrament," 2004. Copyright © 2004, United States Conference of Catholic Bishops, Washington, D.C. All rights reserved. (Quoting Sacred Congregation for Rites, *Eucharisticum mysterium* [On the Worship of the Eucharist], May 25, 1967.)